A RAY OF LIGHT

A BOOK OF SCIENCE AND WONDER

WRITTEN AND PHOTOGRAPHED BY

WALTER WICK

SCHOLASTIC PRESS / NEW YORK

ACKNOWLEDGMENTS

I would like to extend a heartfelt thanks to all my longtime associates at Scholastic, particularly Ellie Berger for her continued support, and especially Ken Geist and David Saylor for their excellent guidance and steady encouragement despite the long wait for this book. I would also like to thank high school physics teachers Peter Moore and Joe Mancino for their experience-based wisdom and enthusiasm for the project from the very beginning; and to Bill Robertson, Professor of Physics & Astronomy at Middle Tennessee State University, for reading the manuscript with a critical eye. Any mistakes that remain are my own. A special thanks to my uniquely talented studio assistant, Heather Aylsworth, and finally, to my wife, Linda Cheverton Wick, for her loving support, and to whom this book is dedicated.

Library of Congress Cataloging-in-Publication Data available

ISBN 978-0-439-16587-7

10 9 8 7 6 5 4 3 2 1   19 20 21 22 23

Printed in China 62

First edition, March 2019

Book design by Walter Wick and Charles Kreloff

PHOTO CREDITS

Page 23 left © 1997 by Walter Wick from the book *A Drop of Water*, published by Scholastic Press, an imprint of Scholastic Inc. Stock photos ©: Page 30 right, Page 31 center, Page 31 top right; Pages 32, 34: NASA; Page 35: Carlos Clarivan/Science Source.

For Linda

And yet how little even the wisest among us know about the nature and work of these bright messengers of the sun as they dart across space!

—ARABELLA B. BUCKLEY,

THE FAIRY-LAND OF SCIENCE, 1878

WHAT IS LIGHT?

Everything from the earth beneath our feet, the water we drink, and the air
we breathe is made of atoms. Atoms are the tiny, invisible building blocks of
matter. Matter can be a solid, liquid, or gas. Matter is the basis of everything
we see, feel, smell, or touch.

What about light? What is it made of? How does it fit alongside everything
else in the world?

LIGHT IS ENERGY

Rub two hands rapidly together and the friction will warm your hands. Strike a wooden match across a rough rock and the friction will cause the phosphor-tipped match to burst into flame. The flame will radiate energy in the form of heat and light as long as there is wood to burn.

Although light is neither a solid, liquid, nor gas, all three kinds of matter can have a role in its creation. Our match has lit the candle, and the melting wax travels up the wick and provides more fuel to the flame. The flame is a violent storm of hydrogen, carbon, and oxygen atoms—large clusters of them breaking down into smaller clusters, releasing energy in the form of heat and light.

INCANDESCENCE

Light that comes from heat is called *incandescence*. A burning candle, red-hot metal, the fiery sun—all are forms of incandescent light. At left, a trickle of electricity heats the coiled metal filament, emitting a soft red glow. As the temperature of an incandescent light source increases, the color of the light emitted shifts from red to orange to white. The color shifts seen below are due to the increasing temperatures of the corresponding light sources pictured above.

Fluorescent, sodium vapor, and light-emitting diodes (LEDs), are some of the many types of light sources not produced from heated substances, so their varying color tints are not connected to temperature. However, all light, no matter how it's produced, is the same form of energy called *electromagnetic radiation*, traveling at the same blazing speed of 186,000 miles per second—a speed so fast that the light from the sun, 93 million miles away, took only eight minutes and twenty seconds to reach the spoon below.

LIGHT WAVES

Light travels in waves. Because waves of all kinds share similar behaviors, we can look to water waves to help us understand the wave behavior of light.

Above, a ball attached to a rod vibrates at three different speeds: slow, medium, and fast. The crest of each wave represents a pulse of energy radiating out from the vibrating ball. The distance between neighboring crests is the *wavelength*. If we think of the ball as a single, vibrating atom, we can imagine light waves emanating from it. Light waves cannot be seen directly. Instead, waves are sensed by the *frequency* of the wave pulses hitting the nerves at the back of our eyes. Longer wavelengths are lower frequency waves, and are perceived as red. Turn up the frequency and the color changes. Medium wavelengths are perceived as green; shorter wavelengths we perceive as blue.

Light waves are not only very fast, but also very small. A distance equal to the width of this pinhead would contain about 6,500 wavelengths of red light, 7,000 of green, and 9,000 of blue. The ability to distinguish these colors is due to our brain's amazing ability to sense the differences between these extremely fast and very tiny pulses of energy.

However, if the distinctly different red, green, and blue wavelengths of light overlap, as we see above, the colors can no longer be distinguished from one another. What we see instead is white light.

A LIGHT OBSTACLE COURSE

Unless obstructed or reflected, light travels in perfectly straight lines. Above, a ray of sunlight comes in straight from the left. Encountering a clear, water-filled box head on, the light remains perfectly straight as it passes through. Arriving at the next box at an angle, the light bends down slightly, then bends up again continuing on a straight path. The bending of light rays by plastic, glass, water, or any other clear substance is called *refraction*.

As fast as light travels, it slows down when going through clear substances, then resumes its faster speed upon entering the air again. Refraction can occur at any point where such speed changes occur. In the example above, refraction is seen at both the air-to-water and water-to-air points of the angled box. At the same time, a portion of light is also reflected away from those points. One of those reflected rays is also refracted again as it exits the box at the top.

When the sunlight enters the triangular box at an angle, the light also refracts downward, just as with the angled rectangular box. But as it leaves the triangle, it angles farther down again. In doing so, you can see that the sunlight has begun to split into its component colors, with those colors appearing ever more distinct and vivid at the far right of the picture. The shorter wavelengths in the blue-violet range of color bend the most, the longer wavelengths of red light bend the least. All other colors fall in between.

THE COLOR SPECTRUM

There are, perhaps, no colors found anywhere on earth as brilliant and vivid as those found in sunlight refracted by a simple glass prism. It should be noted that a photograph, especially those reproduced in a book, cannot fully capture the purity and intensity of color that's observed directly by the human eye.

Here, the full range of the sun's colors are spread out on a piece of paper that has been placed in the path of refracted light. That range of color is called the *color spectrum*, and includes all the colors of the rainbow: red, orange, yellow, green, blue, indigo, and violet. Each color in the spectrum has a different wavelength, and can't be further split by refracting it through another prism.

The color spectrum is the visible portion of a much wider range of electromagnetic radiation. Just beyond the red end of the visible spectrum lies infrared light, which is sensed through our skin as heat. At the other end is ultraviolet light, which, due to its shorter wavelengths, transmits higher energy levels that can damage skin.

LONGER WAVELENGTHS   SHORTER WAVELENGTHS

INFRARED   RED   ORANGE   YELLOW   GREEN   BLUE   INDIGO   VIOLET   ULTRAVIOLET

A VANISHING COLOR TRICK

Overlapping red, green, and blue light will appear as white, but what color is made from overlapping just red and green light? If you're used to getting brown from mixing red and green paint, you may be surprised: red and green light make bright yellow. Mixing green and blue light makes a light blue-green color called cyan. Mixing red and blue light makes magenta.

We now have the basis for a vanishing color trick. Below, two colorful tops on the left are shown spinning on the right. Where did the color go?

Equal amounts of red, green, and blue *or* equal amounts of cyan, magenta, and yellow will result in gray in the spinning tops because no one color dominates, and the eye can no longer discern separate wavelengths when mixed by the rapid motion.

A similar trick is employed in the printing of this book. Though white is obtained from the paper itself, a magnified view of the grays in the tops will reveal a pattern of tiny dots of cyan, magenta, and yellow. By adjusting the balance of those three colors, all the other colors in this book are formed. Digital displays also work this way, except the three base colors are red, green, and blue, and white is obtained by brightening all those colors at once.

 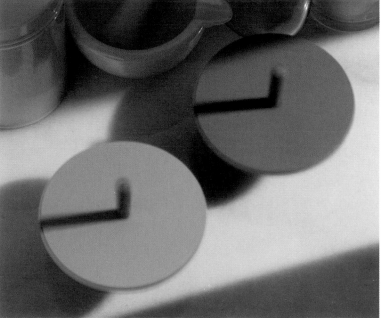

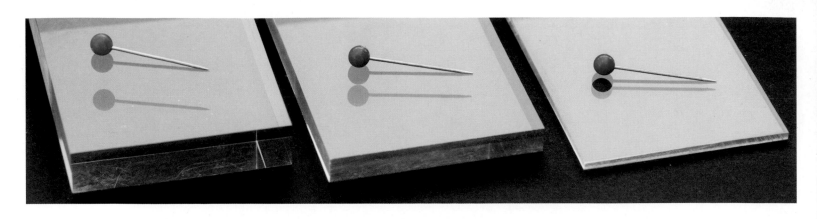

IRIDESCENCE

To the right is a wire frame that has been dipped in a solution of soap and water. Why do we see colors in what is otherwise a clear, colorless liquid? A clue can be found in how objects reflect off both the front and back surfaces of any clear substance.

Soap film becomes extremely thin as it evaporates. As the film thins to dimensions approaching the wavelength of light, wave crests reflecting off the front of the film overlap with wave crests reflecting off the back, much like the overlapping pin reflections on thin glass above. If the double reflection of wave crests of any given wavelength perfectly align, that wavelength's color brightens. At the same time, wave crests of other wavelengths will misalign, inhibiting our ability to see those colors at all. This combination of alignment/misalignment of wave crests is called *interference*. The resulting shimmering color is called *iridescence*. The varying swirl of brilliant colors is due to the ever-changing thickness of the very thin film.

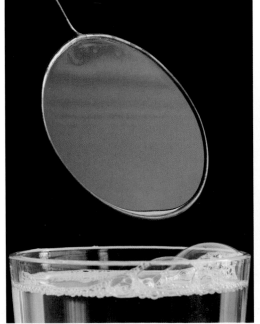

NATURE'S SHIMMERING COLOR

Certain feathers, butterflies, beetles, and shells are examples of iridescence found in living things. Although they may have underlying colors of brown, black, or white, their bright, shimmering surface colors are due to light interacting with microscopic ridges embedded in those surfaces. When light strikes those tiny ridges, a form of interference occurs: certain wavelengths double up and brighten while others cancel out and weaken—much like what we've seen with soap film.

Rainbows are another way nature can split sunlight into its component colors. Because raindrops are spherical, their round shape acts like a lens, focusing a bright spot of sunlight onto the back of the drop. At a certain position in the sky, those bright spots flash colors of the spectrum due to the prism-like refraction occurring inside the drop. Shimmering bright lines of rainbow colors can also be seen at the fringes of refracted light at the bottom of a shallow pool.

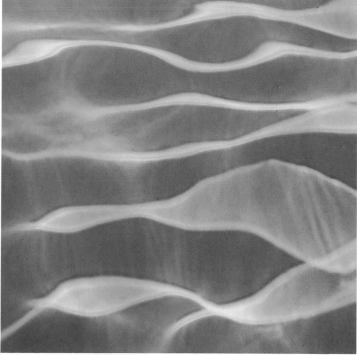

PIGMENTS

Dazzling as the iridescent soap bubble or refracted rainbow are, those colors can flash brilliantly or fade away depending on the angle of the sun, the position of the viewer, and other factors.

Fortunately, much of the color we encounter in the world is due to more permanent materials called *pigments*. From fruit to flowers, from balloons to billboards, pigments produce color by absorbing some wavelengths while scattering others back toward your eye. Chalk is a white pigment because the calcium and oxygen atoms it's composed of scatter most wavelengths. Charcoal is a black pigment because its carbon atoms absorb nearly all wavelengths (converting that absorbed energy to heat).

Pigments, along with related liquefied colorants called *dyes*, can be derived from plants or animals. Many are extracted from the earth. Still others are made from synthetic chemicals.

Though the chemical composition of pigments can be complex, grinding them into fine powder doesn't change how their internal atoms interact with light. The blue pigments above absorb most wavelengths but blue; the yellow pigment absorbs most wavelengths but yellow—even though they are both illuminated by the same light. Suspended in a clear medium such as oil or water, pigments are made into paint, and can be further mixed to make many other colors.

THE LENS

Sunlight is powerful. Streaming in a window you'll feel its warmth, but when a beam of light just five inches wide is focused by a simple lens, the pinpoint concentration of all that energy will cause a match to burst into flame in a matter of seconds.

The human eye refracts light in the same way, which is why you should never stare directly into the sun. The concentration of sunlight will do serious damage to your eyes. The device used here is an ordinary magnifying glass, but used in this way it's a "burning lens." Children should be closely supervised when conducting any experiments involving a burning lens.

The lens above, also an ordinary magnifying glass, is acting much like the human eye, projecting an image of a candle on the wall. The image is upside down, but then so are the images projected onto the back of your eye. Your brain does the work of correcting the upside-down image. Though the candle flame is too hot to touch, very little heat can be felt from the flame's projection.

This arrangement of lens and projection is also the basis of all cameras—whether for stills or video, film or digital—though such cameras require additional lens components to improve image clarity and an enclosure to prevent stray light from washing out the projected image.

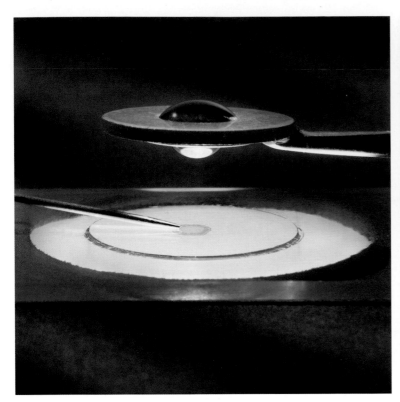
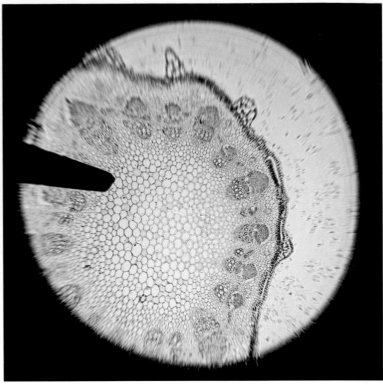

SEEING THE UNSEEN

Simple magnifiers made from lenses have been in use for thousands of years. About 400 years ago, a new way to use those lenses began with the invention of the microscope and telescope, revealing previously unseen wonders: minute structures of plants and animals, mountains on the moon, and new objects in the heavens.

Early microscope lenses were shaped from tiny drops of melted glass, but the lens of the simple microscope above is made with a drop of water suspended in a brass washer. A liquid lens isn't as practical as a solid-glass one, but its steeply curved shape is what enables the lens to focus close in on this slice of sunflower stem—seen here enlarged to fifteen times its actual size.

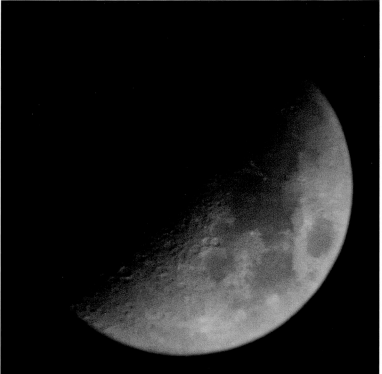

A telescope capable of revealing mountains on the moon can be made with two simple lenses. Above, the nearest lens, called the *eyepiece*, is a strong magnifier bringing light to focus over a very short distance. The furthest lens, called the *objective*, is weaker, and brings light to a focus over a larger distance. This design, usually constructed with two telescoping tubes to hold the lenses, is called a *refracting telescope* because of the light-bending function of the lenses.

The discoveries made with these new optical tools astounded early scientists. Like the examples shown here, early devices provided clarity only in the central portion of the image. But with patience and gradual improvements of the instruments, details of these wonders were carefully mapped and drawn, and a new age of science began.

ATMOSPHERIC LIGHT

Though the same sun illuminates our earth and moon in equal measure, the blue skies and dazzling sunsets visible on earth could never occur on the airless moon.

Light travels fastest in the vacuum of outer space. When it reaches the earth's atmosphere, it slows down a bit, just as it slows further when going from air to water. Oxygen in the upper atmosphere absorbs much of the sun's harmful ultraviolet light. Visible light, meanwhile, is partially scattered by various air molecules. The sky is blue because shorter wavelengths scatter more easily than longer wavelengths. When the sun is low, light must pass through much longer stretches of atmosphere, further scattering blue light, while longer wavelengths of red and orange light slip through, often bathing earth and sky in a golden glow.

The moon's weak gravity accounts for its lack of atmosphere. Sunlight, therefore, reaches its surface unfiltered, resulting in perpetually black skies, extreme temperatures, and dangerously high levels of radiation.

EARTH AND MOON SIZE COMPARISON

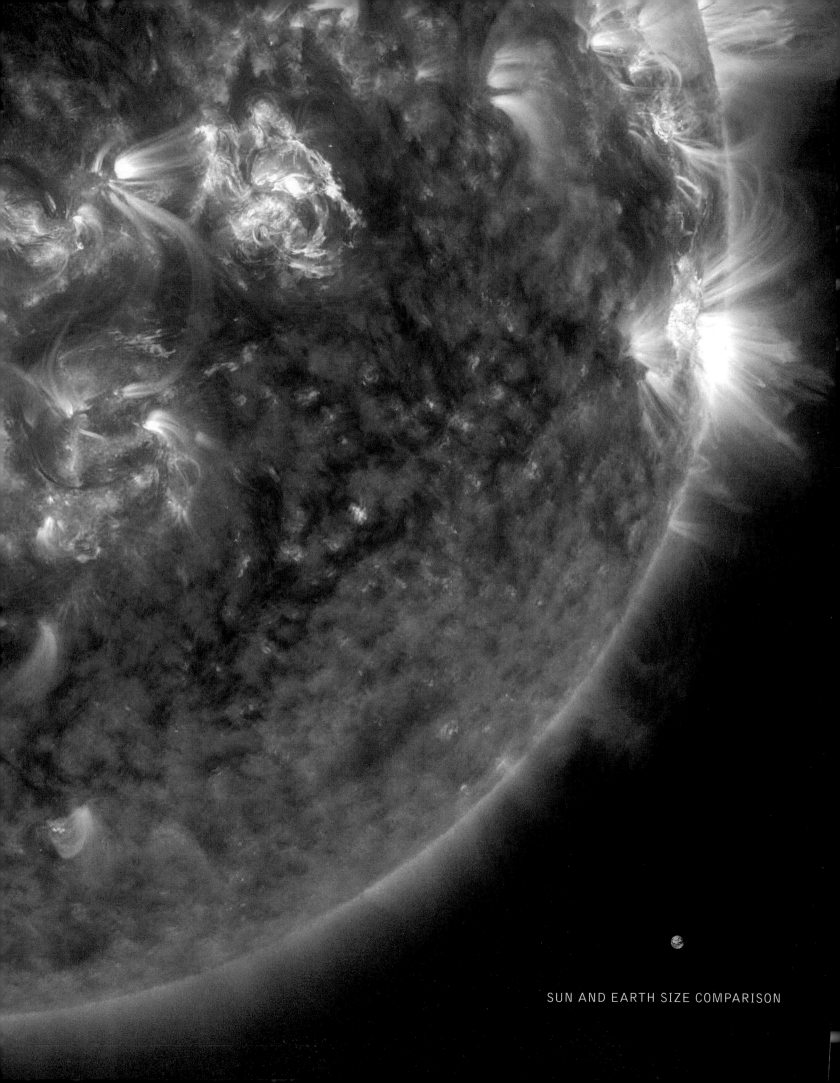

SUN AND EARTH SIZE COMPARISON

THE SUN

The sun is so massive, a million earths could fit inside it. Its gravity is so strong, extreme pressure at its center fuses together hydrogen atoms, transforming them into helium. This transformation of hydrogen to helium—the two main components of the sun—is called *nuclear fusion*, a process that results in the release of enormous amounts of energy—the visible portion of which we call light.

The earth's distance of 93 million miles helps keep us safe from the sun's ferocious heat. If the earth were the size of the blue pin shown below, the sun would be the size of a seventeen-inch ball. At that scale, a string 150 feet long would represent the distance from the sun to the earth. If you were to place the ball at the center of a soccer field and walk around it with the pin, you would simulate the earth's orbit around the sun. In doing so, with every step you could sense how the earth receives only a tiny portion of the sun's enormous outpouring of energy.

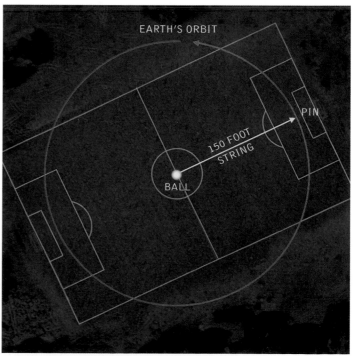

EARTH, SUN, STARS COMPOSITE

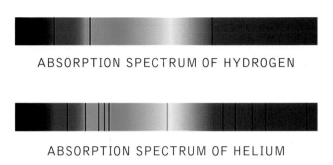

ABSORPTION SPECTRUM OF HYDROGEN

ABSORPTION SPECTRUM OF HELIUM

BRIGHT MESSENGERS

Given the sun's great distance from earth, how could we possibly know what it's made of? The answer can be found hidden in plain sight.

When sunlight is refracted by a prism, we see a continuous color spectrum. When refracted by an instrument called a *spectroscope*, a pattern of dark lines reveals gaps in the spectrum. While spectrum colors represent light emitted by atoms, the gaps represent light absorbed by those atoms. Such patterns, like that of hydrogen and helium shown above, are unique to different atoms. Thus, like coded messages, these patterns carried along within light itself tell us not only what the sun is made of—but what other stars are made of, too.

EVERY RAY OF LIGHT

The last rays of summer light stream through a window. A tiny blue earth makes its yearlong orbit around the sun, a journey nearly 600 million miles long. The earth rotates daily in its orbit, turning toward the sun each morning, turning away again at night. Each day, the earth takes the littlest sips of the sun's vast outpouring of energy. However tiny that portion of light is that reaches us, we could not exist without its life-sustaining energy—darting across space, quivering within each and every ray of light.

SPECTRUM OF ELECTROMAGNETIC RADIATION

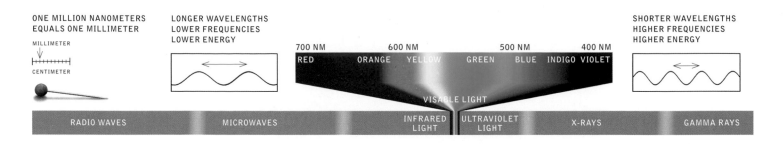

ONE MILLION NANOMETERS
EQUALS ONE MILLIMETER

MILLIMETER

CENTIMETER

LONGER WAVELENGTHS
LOWER FREQUENCIES
LOWER ENERGY

SHORTER WAVELENGTHS
HIGHER FREQUENCIES
HIGHER ENERGY

700 NM   600 NM   500 NM   400 NM
RED   ORANGE   YELLOW   GREEN   BLUE   INDIGO VIOLET

VISABLE LIGHT

RADIO WAVES   MICROWAVES   INFRARED LIGHT | ULTRAVIOLET LIGHT   X-RAYS   GAMMA RAYS

Visible light occupies a tiny region of a much larger range of electromagnetic radiation. Light waves are measured in nanometers (1 millionth of a millimeter). Red light, at about 620–700 nanometers (nm), are the longest wavelengths of the visible spectrum, while violet, at around 400–450 nm, are the shortest wavelengths we can see. With shorter wavelengths, wave crests arrive with greater frequency, therefore are higher energy waves. Because all waves travel at the same speed in a vacuum, any wave can be described by the distance between two wave crests or by the frequency of those waves. Low frequency radio waves can be miles long between crests; high frequency gamma rays can be smaller than the size of an atom.

NOTES ON THE SCIENCE AND EXPERIMENTS

This book's emphasis on visual presentation over complex text necessitates excluding certain details about the science depicted and methods used for experiments. For the benefit of the more advanced or curious reader, extra detail will be found in the notes that follow.

WHAT IS LIGHT?

While just over 100 different kinds of atoms are known, carbon, hydrogen, oxygen, and nitrogen are the most common. Together with sulphur and phosphor, these atoms are the basis for most life on earth. The central core of an atom is called a *nucleus*. The nucleus is surrounded by one or more electrons in a perpetual state of motion. The number of electrons of a given atom is what distinguishes atoms one from another. For example, hydrogen has one electron, while carbon has six, and oxygen eight. When light is emitted from atoms, electrons are pulled closer to the nucleus; when light is absorbed, the electrons are pushed farther from the nucleus. Atoms are most often found clustered in discrete groupings, or *molecules*. Molecules, in turn, cluster in a multitude of ways to form the earth's endless variety of substances. Still, it's the enormous jumble of atoms within those substances that are the principal receptors and emitters of light.

LIGHT IS ENERGY

Candlelight derives its fuel from wax, a compound composed of hydrocarbon molecules, named for the hydrogen and carbon atoms they contain. Heat from the flame breaks down these large molecules, which then combine with oxygen from the air to reform as smaller carbon dioxide and water molecules, releasing light energy in the process.

INCANDESCENCE

The correlation between heated substances and color of light emitted is called *color temperature*, and is measured in Kelvin (K), a temperature scale named for its discoverer.

Though incandescent light emits all colors of the spectrum, red dominates in the lower temperature range, while blue increases with higher temperatures. For example, the reddish glow of a candle is 1,850K, a household tungsten bulb at 2,700K is yellowish, while sunlight, at 5,500K, is mixed with enough blue to make it appear white. Light not produced by heated substances falls under a broad category known as *luminescence*, and would include fluorescent, sodium vapor, and LED lights. Such sources produce light that has large gaps in the color spectrum and can have tints of green, yellow, or blue as a result.

LIGHT WAVES

While water waves are one way to simulate the wave behavior of light, it has its limitations. A ball vibrating on the water's surface sends out waves in two dimensions, while light radiates out in three dimensions. Also, light has dual behavior, that is, there are times when it's more convenient to describe light not in terms of waves, but as particles called *photons*. Photons are discrete packets of energy with no physical mass. They travel at the speed of light, and affect brightness and color by their frequency and the amount of energy contained within each photon. In science, there is no dispute over the question of whether light is made of waves or particles, it's both: a characteristic known as the *wave-particle duality*.

A LIGHT OBSTACLE COURSE

For this experiment, a mirror placed outdoors was used to redirect sunlight through a window. The water-filled boxes were constructed from 1/8" acrylic, and a few grains of powdered milk provided enough suspended particles to make light rays visible in the water. Solid shapes of glass or clear plastic would work for this experiment, too, but the degree with which light is bent may differ. Such differences in the light-bending properties is called the *refractive index*. High-quality camera lenses would not be possible without lens components of differing refractive indices.

THE COLOR SPECTRUM

This prism is glass. A mirror was used to redirect sunlight from outside. The cardboard slot is about 1/8" inch wide, but narrower slots work well, too. A white card is angled along the path of light exiting from the prism for better visibility of spectrum colors.

A VANISHING COLOR TRICK

Three separate spotlights, equipped with 3,200K tungsten bulbs, were filtered with red-, green-, and blue-colored gels and projected in overlapping circles on the wall. In cameras and digital displays, red, green, and blue are considered primary colors, because they serve as the basis from which all other colors are made with those devices.

An inkjet printer was used to make the tops' colors, but required a certain amount of trial and error to get both sets of color to appear gray when spinning. If any one color was too dark, the gray would be tinted by a combination of the two other dominant colors.

In printed books such as this one, tiny dots of cyan, magenta, and yellow are accompanied by dots of black ink, too. This method is referred to as CMYK printing, with the letter "K" referring to the color black. Despite the presence of black, neutral gray and black tones in the book usually include dots of CMY colors as well.

IRIDESCENCE

When the wave crests align, it's called *constructive interference* because it reinforces, or amplifies a particular color. When the wave crests misalign, it's called *destructive interference* because the misaligned crests imitate non-visible wavelengths, so no color is visible. Water coated with oil often becomes iridescent due to interference of light reflecting on the front and back surfaces of the extremely thin film of oil floating on top of the water.

NATURE'S SHIMMERING COLOR

Interference due to microscopic structures is called *structural coloration*. Interference also occurs when light passes through or reflects off glass or plastic that has been etched with a series of fine parallel lines. When light interacts with those lines, it *diffracts*, or spreads out, interfering with light diffracting from neighboring lines, resulting in a rainbow effect. Such patterns, called *diffraction gratings*, are used in everything from light-analysis instruments, such as spectroscopes, to common holographic foils and plastics.

PIGMENTS

As we've seen with projected light, red light mixed with green makes yellow, and that yellow mixed with blue light makes white. Mixing colored light is called *additive color*, because you're adding one wavelength of light to another. Mixing paint, on the other hand, is called *subtractive color*, because a mixture of blue and yellow paint, for example, absorbs light of both pigments, resulting not in white, but green.

THE LENS/SEEING THE UNSEEN

In combination with bright sunlight, any magnifying glass can be turned into a "burning lens." It can't be emphasized enough that care should be taken when using a lens in this way. A large-diameter lens will concentrate more light energy and will burn hotter as a result.

The distance between a lens and the sharply focused image of a distant object is called the *focal length*. It's the curvature of the lens, not the diameter, that determines focal length. The focal length of the lens on page 26 is 300mm, and its diameter is 100mm. The lens on page 27 has a focal length of 100mm, and a diameter of 50mm.

The hole in the washer that holds the water lens is 1/4", and could suspend one to three drops. More water made the lens more bulbous, which in turn provided greater magnification. Any thin, waterproof material, such as plastic, could be used to make a water microscope. A smooth, round hole from 1/8" to 1/4" would do. It's best if the specimen be well lit, and the eye needs to be very close to the drop.

THE SUN

Unlike a candle flame, where light is released when large molecules are broken down into smaller ones, the sun's energy comes from the sun's core, where hydrogen atoms are fused together under enormous pressure, converting them to helium. The temperature at the center of the sun's core is about 15 million Kelvin, but by the time that heat reaches the sun's surface it drops to about 5,800K.

BRIGHT MESSENGERS

In photographs of earth taken from space, stars are usually not visible due to the extremes of light and dark. To illustrate the relative position of earth and sun, and that stars are present in all directions, the picture on page 34 is a composite of separate photographs of earth, sun, and stars.

While the sun is 93 million miles away from earth, other stars are so much more distant that they are measured in *light-years*—the distance light travels in a year. The nearest stars are just over four light-years away; the farthest stars are some 13 billion light-years distant. Yet, despite such unimaginable stretches of space, light still manages to reach us, bringing with it clues to what the stars are made of.

ABOUT THIS BOOK

This book was conceived as a companion to my 1997 book *A Drop of Water: A Book of Science and Wonder*, although I could not have imagined then that it would take two decades to bring it to fruition. In those intervening years, however, I created many other books for children that had the benefit of further reinforcing what I had already begun to see firsthand: the astounding visual acuity of young readers. Thus encouraged, I took a leap of faith that I could tackle the complex subject of light by way of tangible, concrete table-top experiments, with the hope that the intrinsic wonders of this topic would feel as close to my readers as the book they hold in their hands.

The photographs are of experiments set up in my studio and environs (with the exception of a few) and were made with a digital camera. Some images required combining two or more exposures for balancing light levels or color, others required some localized retouching for clarity, but all are faithful to the phenomena described in the text.

—WALTER WICK